GIFT FROM AN ANGEL

Other Titles by Eileen Goble

Spirit Guides - A journey through myth to reality

Rainbow Meditation - Inner Direction and Healing
(Audio cassette with 20 page colour interpretation booklet)

Rainbow Meditation - Change and Growth
(Audio Cassette with 20 page colour interpretation booklet)

White Light Meditation (Audio Cassette)

GIFT FROM AN ANGEL

Eileen Goble

THE HOLISTIC CENTRE
Melbourne, Australia

Published in 1996 by:
The Holistic Centre
55 Marianne Way, Mt.Waverley Vic. 3149. Australia.

Copyright Eileen Goble 1996

Printed in Melbourne by:
Australian Print Group.

Cover by Andrew Bradsworth
Bradsworth Design, Melbourne

Edited by: Julia Wilson

ISBN: 0 9586570 0 9
National Library of Australia

International Distributors:
New Zealand: Peaceful Living, Tauranga
United Kingdom: L.N. Fowler & Co. Ltd., Essex

This book is sold subject to the condition that it shall not by way
of trade or otherwise, be lent, re-sold, hired out, or otherwise
circulated without the publisher's prior consent in any form of
binding or cover other than that in which it is published and
without a similar condition including this condition being
imposed on the subsequent purchaser.

DEDICATION

To *Mary* who entrusted these beautiful channelled messages to my care.

All names used in this book have been changed to protect the identity of the people concerned.

Mary's Gift

It was just after midday, on a beautiful sunny spring day, whilst driving on a straight stretch of road in country Victoria, that my friend Mary died. A seemingly impossible accident between the only two vehicles on the highway. An unexpected phone call had brought us together. An unexpected phone call from her sister informed me of her death.

The period between those two phone calls covered less than two years, but the growth and learning we both experienced could have spanned many lifetimes. To say that Mary was important to my spiritual growth is to undervalue the impact we had on each other. We were instrumental in an awakening of the spirit that may have taken us eons to achieve individually.

The news of her death left me numb. Denial was strong within me. I had been talking to Mary just two days before when I had given her a book I felt she needed at that time. A book about self-empowerment. She read it almost immediately, then rang to say it had answered all her questions - she now knew what she was going to do for the rest of her life. A few hours later she was gone. It did not seem to make sense.

Over the next few days I reflected on what we had learnt since our first meeting. How her migraines had initiated her first consultation with me, and how it later became apparent that they were just the catalyst to bring us together. How through her trust in me coupled with my inherent curiosity we explored her emerging natural ability to be a trance medium. The significant aspects of this period I have already recounted in my first book, *Spirit Guides*.

All those memories came flooding back to me adding to my grief and sense of loss. It was many days later that I remembered that when I last saw Mary she gave me an exercise book with some trance channelled writings she had recently received. Mary told me she felt that the writings were to be given to me. She was told by her angels that I would know what to do with them.

I assumed that I was meant to type them up, because the writing was difficult to read, however when I got around to transcribing them, many months later, I began to realise why she had given it to me. I was to share it with others. It is an expression of unconditional love. A source of inspiration and motivation for the soul that wishes to grow. It is with love that this gift is now offered to you. Please take from these words of wisdom what you need, knowing that they come from the source of all light.

To appreciate the significance of this gift, this inheritance as it has now become, you perhaps need to understand Mary.

She was brought up in a strong catholic family, the last of 13 children. They were poor but proud with strong family ties. However her childhood was marked with many abusive situations. As the youngest child with two older brothers who betrayed her trust, an alcoholic father and insufficient supervision from a mother burdened by a large family, Mary was very vulnerable. She developed feelings of guilt, blame and unworthiness. Because she never shared all those painful memories with anyone but myself, it took until our coming together to release the negative belief systems attached to this period of her life.

Mary had many children of her own and such was the depth of her belief in the sanctity of motherhood, that she carried enormous guilt when compelled to have a hysterectomy. This and the loss of a stillborn son were the basis of the migraines that first brought her to me for help..

During our time together we worked through the guilt and sense of unworthiness that had been a hallmark of her life. Through the therapy I could offer, and the wisdom that she was receiving from her angels of light, she became more accepting of herself allowing the true dignity of the spirit to shine through. She was finally able to forgive those who had caused her pain and release the memories she no longer needed.

Her devotion to her catholic faith remained throughout her life and she found no conflict between that and the emergence of her ability to channel the guides and angels who made their presence known to her. Her family were not always comfortable with her clairvoyance but to her it was but an extension of the spiritual life she embraced.

When I first met Mary she was confused, hurting and totally unaware of her own self empowerment. She was also honest, caring of everybody but herself and a good listener. These qualities enabled her to receive the healing and guidance in an almost child-like state of trust.

As she became more in tune with her own self, she began to assert her needs a little more, was less likely to be dissuaded from doing what she really wanted and more likely to offer advice rather than just listen. All this change and growth caused quite a lot of discomfort amongst her family and friends. They were used to a Mary they could influence and could not quite reconcile themselves to this new Mary who seemed to know her own mind.

Mary came to me one day saying, "The strangest thing happened last night." She went on to explain that she had been invited to a barbeque that was being given to welcome some visiting evangelists to town. One of Mary's close friends was the host. She related to me that one of the young men took her aside and started to ask her a lot of questions about what she was doing and did she know that communicating with spirits was the devil's work.

She went on to say, "As I was trying to explain to him that what I was doing was not wrong I realised that the words coming out of my mouth were not my thoughts but what I was saying made sense. The next thing I realised it was half an hour later and the young man was thanking me for sharing my thoughts with him. I had no real idea what I had been saying for all that time but he had stopped being aggressive and wished me best wishes for the future."

We discussed what had happened and realised that her friends had been concerned about the changes in Mary and attempted to influence her by encouraging the young evangelist to question her motives. However, her angels of light had taken over and helped her find the words to put this young man's mind at rest. This was the first recognised instance of spontaneous trance channelling for Mary and highlighted the protection and support her guides were offering her. It was also an indication of how her family and friends felt about her emerging spiritual self.

After this instance she became more confident and positive whenever people came to her for help and advice. And come to her they did. However she also went out of her way to be there for people in need. She started working as a home-help and whilst doing the housework would listen to the needs of the person she was helping. She would often go back in her own time and sit and have a *cuppa* with them and invariably her angels would come through offering just the right advice needed at that time.

Her angels would come to her at night and take her on incredible journeys to show her the spiritual realm. She was telling me one day about being taken to a beautiful place and being escorted into a big room. Her first impression was of an image of Jesus standing at the door welcoming her and being overwhelmed with the love emanating from his aura. Then he seemed to be drawing her attention to a group of people sitting at a large round table.

She became aware that some of the faces were

familiar and realised that all had been leaders of countries, religious organisations or dynasties when they were alive. They were from various races and different times in history. They were focused on an image of the earth in the centre of the table and seemed to be discussing what to do next. The impression given to her was that they were all working for world peace, even though when alive they may have been enemies. They were now working together to bring peace to the earth. It made a rather odd picture with such diverse cultures coming together, but strangely comforting in the thought it evoked.

Mary questioned why she had been shown this and what she could do to help. The response she got was, "Love yourself then share this love with others. Peace can be yours for all time". The experience was quite overwhelming, but helped her to understand the need for love in the world. She also now understood that help was being offered from those entities who had had such an influence in world affairs when they were alive. A feeling of them now wanting to restore peace where they had been influential in creating disharmony when alive. I guess you could call it balancing the books. Karma.

On another occasion Mary was shown some of her past lives, particularly those we had shared. Some we knew about because of our own exploration in this area, but the one they particularly wanted to show her was of a time in ancient China when I had been a *healer* and she was brought to me by her grandmother for help. She had refused my help in those days and had died. The message they were conveying to her was that she had been given the opportunity to seek my help in this lifetime and she had accepted it despite not knowing anything about me or what I did.

We discussed the relevance of this information and realised that it is not the type of therapy or help that you seek but your acceptance of the help offered. The power to heal is in the asking and accepting not in the technicality of the process. A sobering thought, one that demands that judgement and ego has no place in healing and growth.

Her angels of light often asked Mary to help them with spirits who were having trouble making the transition from the earth plane to the spiritual realm. She would invariably be awakened at night to *rescue* lost souls and earthbounds. Souls who could not find their way to the light either through their own negative thought patterns or confusion about where they were.

Whilst her generous nature ensured that she would never refuse a request to help these souls in need, she did not really enjoy experiencing their pain. Because of her now heightened sensitivity she was able to feel what they were feeling, and her desire to help was such that she would take it on willingly. Her guides patiently encouraged her to respect her own self by helping without taking on their pain.

The episode that really got this message across was when she was asked to help two souls in urgent need. A woman and her child had been holidaying in a caravan on the banks of a nearby river. She had left her husband because they were having marriage difficulties. She needed a break and had taken the offer of a holiday in a friend's caravan. Her husband had found her and demanded she return home. The argument became heated and got out of hand. He shot them both, set the caravan alight and then shot himself, incinerating all three of them.

The woman and child were still stuck in the flames unable to realise what had happened to them. They were in spiritual shock. Mary was asked to help them find their way to the light. However she took on the feeling of being caught in the fire and the experience was too much for her. She was unable to help at that time. She came to me in great distress the following day devastated that she had not been able to help and concerned that the woman and child were still burning.

I reassured her that because there is no time in the spiritual world we would be able to complete the rescue now and the woman's suffering, if any, would cease to exist in her memory. I explained to Mary that as the woman and child had left their physical bodies they could no longer feel pain, but would probably be in a state of confusion.

Reassured Mary again tapped into that image of the woman and child and I was able to guide her to communicate with the woman without becoming her. Between Mary's fear of feeling the heat of the flames again, and the confusion within the spirit of the woman who was earthbound, it took a lot of positive forceful encouragement and specific guidance to complete the process of rescuing these two lost souls.

The lesson Mary learned from this stood her in good stead whenever asked to assist in a rescue again. She now fully appreciated the need to stay focused within herself and separate from whatever another soul has chosen to experience. She realised the need to care for herself at all times, as she was the only one responsible for her own well-being. Interestingly, after that episode she was not asked to help in many more rescues. It appeared to be that now she had learned that valuable lesson she could move onto other forms of learning. She had obviously graduated to the next class.

Mary's love for her mother was totally unconditional. This was reflected in the importance she placed on motherhood and the years she spent caring for her mother until she died after years of suffering. Mary mourned the loss of her mother even though it liberated her from the onerous task of nursing her whilst rearing her six surviving children.

However this unconditional love was not extended to the males who came into her life and this proved to be one of the last challenges she faced. Whilst she loved all her sons, her relationship with her brothers, father and even husband was quite judgemental. It was partially understandable when the abusive childhood was taken into consideration, but the premise became confused when we reflected on the fact that out of the seven children she bore, six were males. We spent a lot of time discussing why she had invited such a diverse number of male relationships into her life.

Part of her therapy was to investigate the past lives that had brought this challenge into this lifetime. We found that she had spent quite a few lifetimes suffering from abuse, generally as a female at the hands of males. This took many forms, and through lifetimes in a vast array of cultures and religious beliefs. It seemed to me that she had been punishing herself for a long time and for what?

I realised that before she could release this

pattern of suffering we would need to find out what she had done in the past and had judged to be so objectionable that she deserved such punishment. This was something Mary did not want to look at, but realised she would need to acknowledge if this cycle of self-punishment was to end and not be carried over into the next lifetime.

It came about that I was given information during a meditation session with my guides. Mary had been the son of a village chief in a lifetime over two thousand years ago. There was an abuse of power by him and a life of indulgence and sexual excesses with the women for whom he was responsible. These were not family members but women whose lives were under his care.

His father discovered his abusive behaviour and was so ashamed of him that he disinherited him and expelled him from the community. The son's shame on realising his disgrace was such that he committed suicide.

After death the son was still carrying the shame; it had not been absolved by the suicide and it is this shame that had been the motivating force behind Mary's lifetime after lifetime of abuse and punishment at the hands of males. She had been trying to absolve herself of the shame and guilt she had imposed upon herself. The feelings she felt towards her brothers, father and husband were just a reflection of the judgement she had placed upon herself so many years ago. The son who had betrayed the trust placed in him by the father. She judged all men the same as she had judged herself.

Whilst horrified at her actions in that lifetime, Mary expressed that she had had enough punishment and it was time she released the shame and got on with her life. Through therapy I helped her face that man she had been so long ago and to realise that he was just another soul on a journey of learning and deserving of forgiveness the same as everybody else. She was eventually able to forgive and therefore able to release that past life essence of herself and consequently release herself from continual punishment.

The next time Mary saw her brothers she was astounded at the difference in her attitude towards them. She was even able to speak to them, something she had avoided for many years. She had compassion for them, because their lives had mirrored their father's and they were in need of help themselves. She was able to tell them that she forgave them for their behaviour towards her during childhood..

It was a short time after this that Mary received the channelled message from her angels which is now being shared with you and was finally able to see the need for true unconditional forgiveness of the self.

For as you truly forgive yourself, then forgiveness of others becomes a natural extension of that loving energy.

Reflecting upon her death, I realised that forgiving herself of those past life actions had been the prime purpose of her life this time round. Having achieved her objective she was free to go. The book I gave her just before her death was about self-empowerment; being yourself in all situations. I cannot remember the title and obviously it does not matter because it was not for me but for Mary. It was what she needed to read to enable her to recognise that she had truly moved into a new stage of her spiritual growth. It was not a conscious decision to have that car accident but the spirit realising that the purpose of the life had been completed and that it was time to *go home*.

Recognising why she had gone did not immediately diminish my great sense of loss and even anger. However my grief only lasted as long as it took me to realise that the greatest gift I could give to Mary was to accept her decision to go and that I must continue without her.

My own growth has been enormous since that time and in a sense I too was liberated from our period of intense learning. I moved into the next stage of my own spiritual development: that of sharing all that I have learned and helping others with the wisdom and tools that I have been given.

As part of the on-going process of helping others I have included at the end of this book a meditation that you can use to contact your angels. This is my gift to you all.

Accept this book of channelled writing from the angels in the same way that it was received by Mary - with an openness of heart and spirit. Let it be an inspiration to you. You can read it in its entirety or select a page at random as a focus of insight or meditation. You will find that if you need advice from your angels you can open any page and there will be your answer.

However you may choose to use this gift of love, know that you are always surrounded by your angels of light and their love is boundless. You are never alone, you are never without love, you are never without support in your every endeavour.

Let love and light be your guide.

Eileen Goble

Open your heart to the light and darkness will soon disperse. Just remember, to recognize the light. Through darkness you must travel. Learn as you go then you can give to others the key of happiness.

While you are in the master's presence all anger and resentment dissolve. You become filled with love and peace, then you are uplifted, your consciousness raises you above the pulls and antagonisms of the earthly plane, so my child feel at peace.

The true light is a gentle love, swelling within you, enabling you to look on the world with love, understanding and respect. As you learn to respect the soul of your fellow man, you respect his life in every way. Thus gentle spirit, the respect for one another must come. For my child this is the generation of the one true light and the true light is that of love.

If you find things not falling into place, delays and oppositions in your way, know for sure you are being prepared, be patient as you are preparing for a greater initiation. Without patience no great or good work can be accomplished.

Every single detail of a soul's work must be done perfectly. So do be patient in your work with all the happenings in your daily life, be patient and especially patient with your fellow man.

*K*now that in the mind of God is the picture of perfect man His children, Christ, You! To God you are not weak nor are you the erring child of earth. God holds you forever as the perfect form. His thought, the Christ Man, created in His image.

Remain steadfast on the path on which your feet have been quieted there lies the treasure of life the never ending stream of help, healing and happiness. Your angels and brothers are on the road with you. You know you have only to ask in simple trust and you shall receive. Your every need is always catered for.

My child loving is living in God, so is it activity in God, as you are but a spark of God. So each thought and action is of God not of the world. When you love in God you no longer respond to the lower vibrations of death and destruction, but those of true and abundant life.

*T*he one true sustenance, the greatest restraining power that all mankind is able to receive is the strength from God. So my child if you feel illness of the human flesh, weariness in mind, despondence and hopelessness, quiet yourself and turn your thoughts away from yourself, focus yourself, the oneself, in God.

Do not falter, do not waver, hold fast to the belief in the Greatest White Spirit, be directed by the light and you will find all your needs taken care of.

Be true this is the essence of the spiritual life. Always ring true for the note of the spirit is sounded on the higher planes all the knocks and tribulations you receive are but to test you, to see if you can ring true. To ring true you must respond with all the goodness that is within you.

Remain in contact with your higher self forever pulling yourself up to the mark. Putting aside the claims below your higher self, overcomes the pulling of your lower self. Continue to give joyously to mankind, help them to keep in contact with the greater part of them, their higher self.

Remember my child first you are spirit second body. Let your spirit shine for man to see and recognize the real you.

Let me tell you this, the greatest claim upon you is that of God, be it of your spirit or in other words your highest self. The one true self is the shining spirit. To this you must be true above all things. Do not let anything draw you from attaining your soul's true pursuit of breath and light and eternal love.

The best way to pray or meditate is to place yourself in attunement completely with the spirit of love. Be in it, of it, live in it. Do not dwell constantly on mundane things but of God.

Of yourself as a physical being, you are but a pebble but when you dwell in the centre of the heavenly light you become great. For there you are consciously with God for God is within you, of you, and all things work together for the good, when you are good, feel good, be good, as within God.

*M*y dear child each and every soul must withstand great pressure and become well tested for what if the master spirit calls you for important work involving many souls, and what if you had not been tested and proved. Is it not possible you would break down under the stress of the work? What I tell you is this, we are helping you in your endeavour to follow the path of light, withstanding all testing and disappointments.

Such a glorious chance stretches out before you. The disappointments, trouble, trivialities of each day, the annoyances, the hurts which you allow yourself to feel coming from daily life, are all but small, though you allow yourself to see them as big. Let them go, let them fade, concentrate my love on the eternal love, become as a child. Surrender your self will to divine love.

My child there be not death nor need your flesh be weary, for when the soul enters the full glory of the Almighty One, there is no weariness. May the life giver dispel all tiredness and weariness with eternal love.

*M*y child show forth your childlike faith put your hand in that of the master. This is the hand of truth it is security it will never let you down. Earthly men may fail you but never your master.

If you should seek your master you will find him. You will hear his voice when he speaks to you, once you overcome the lower self and learn to think and speak as your higher self.

Should you feel tired and weary, place yourself in the golden light surround your soul in love. Feel the gentle beauty surround you, feel refreshed. Keep certain contact with the highest one, nothing can go wrong.

Do not worry about decisions, whether to do this, that or the other. As your decisions will be made easy for you if you remain awakened to the spirit. Respond to the gentle guidance put at your disposal, the gentle guidance ever present within you.

Follow the light as it breaks in your heart, obey the voice of your inner spirit, do that which rings true.

The power within the heart can reduce negative into positive, darkness to light, then the inflowing light will produce health because it produces harmony.

Do not concentrate on disease and darkness, concentrate on harmony and light. Concentrate on being in the centre of the spirit, the centre of the master will overcome you, then the weariness of the flesh will fall away by your inner effort of changing the dark atoms into light.

Live always in the light there need be no healing from outside for the light itself will heal you.

Do learn to become aware of the ever presence of the master. He is always there, even in the biggest crowd you can centre your thoughts and remain mindful of his presence. You do not need to be in solitude to feel his presence.

There is no thought nor action that escapes the notice of your master, but he is not a judge, he judges not, he only knows love and deep compassion blended with understanding. Remember then to call on him then you can learn to look on all others with the same gentle love shown to you.

If another's actions disturbs you, irritates you and you hurt from injustice, do not try to attack with your thoughts the one who offends you. Remember to give yourself to the master of love. There can be no compromise, your way has been clearly shown being the way of love, patience, gentleness and peace.

Love's true emotion is that of light. When thinking of the suffering of the world you can send off a great light of love if you look at it appropriately in a positive manner not with depression, and a great light will descend into the centre of the weary hearts, the sad and sick will be uplifted in time or new life and body will be created.

Let go, surrender - lay down your problems, do not try to unravel the knots, it only gets tighter as you pull it. Let it go, concentrate with all your heart on love, knowing the knot will be unravelled if you stand back. Fill yourself with love and ask truly for guidance, your problems will be solved.

Surrender your thoughts to love. Knowing the true light and love is continually demonstrated throughout life. For if you live in accordance with spiritual law you will harm no man nor will any man truly harm you, for you will see above his actions.

Your master takes notice of each and every effort you make understanding each and every failure, and all your triumphs. Continually he pours forth his love on you. Tell me - if he who is so beautiful and grand in spirit continues pouring love on you, in spite of your downfalls, can it be so hard on you to send a little love to your fellow man, in fact all living things.

My child there is so much to learn, so much for you to pass on. Divorcing yourself from wisdom, divorces yourself from love. Learn to distinguish between love, true impartial and compassionate love, and emotionalism that can sweep you off your feet and destroy you.

Loving is giving the highest and truest within you to your fellow man. To love is to give the best light from your spirit, the true white light, this is love.

Applying love by your inner attitude towards any human problem is solving all difficulties, all problems, all misunderstandings. Step aside from your calculating mind, just let divine love operate in you.

Send forth from your inner self God's love. You will be surprised to find how your problems will be solved, the knots unloosened. Where there is love there can be no separation not even in death, death is but a transition.

So you come across some difficulties and personal hurts, attune yourself to greater heights. Visualize the form of the golden one in the white light. Holding that vision, think of the one that harms or hurts you or with whom you feel at variance. A shaft of light will go to him, there will be a change in the position and things will go smoothly, the crooked planes made straight. But remember my child give yourself completely to the light.

*W*ise men do not argue, they remain silent and move quietly on their path concerned only with learning and following the master's footsteps. Remember you yourself must work in everyday life and it is your reactions to daily events and conditions of life that can bring about attunement and achievement.

It is not good enough to just listen to your master or any angel or teacher unless you are willing to work for self mastery. The beginning is being aware of the quiet voice within each and everyone of you, the gradually increasing light that causes you to react as a gentle being to all conditions of life and all circumstances. Listen and be aware.

Loving is to give and show the God spirit within, without any thought of return. One is so apt to expect a return for the love you give, but remember that the soul must first learn of love. Love is the inner beauty that flows from the heart, from love itself, so let it rule.

There is nothing to fear but fear itself. Fear is man's darkest enemy and the last to be overthrown, so have no fear. Do your best, nothing else is asked of you, resigning all to the wisdom and love embodied in the Divine law. Be true, sincere, faithful and loving in your human relationships. Let love rule your heart and life.

One cannot give love until it is recognised in oneself. This does not mean being selfish, it means being kind to yourself. Make opportunities in your daily routine for the Christ love to shine forth. This is what is meant by loving yourself. Love peace of mind by doing the right thing, love living within the Divine law.

Ah, my children to forgive totally is often most difficult, but by forgiving you release the spirit, the soul that has been kept in bondage, tied to a stake. Increase beauty on earth by responding to love and beauty so decreasing the darkness from the other side, the darkness and ignorance, bitterness and selfishness of humanity.

One may ask just how do we walk the spiritual path, my child listen: you say little, love much, give all, judge no man, respond to all that is good and follow your lead.

By now you must be ready to act as you learn, so live each day so that you at all times act as a being of love; this is not sentimentality. Love is seeing good, recognizing the divine law of cause and effect, that which works throughout life. Love is being tolerant towards all men and daily happenings, to be patient, kind and meek. All these qualities can be found in but one word, love.

The surface is but a shell, look beyond, do not judge by what you see, develop an inner vision and insight to cause and effect. You will then know you cannot judge any man.

Remember well that you too need forgiveness, learn to forgive freely, judging not. You know not any soul but your duty is to forgive, it is your surpassing joy to be the divine spark in all men.

Believe there is always something beautiful to be found if you but look for it. Concentrate on this, not the reverse. This is the divine magic we are endeavouring to reveal unto you, help you to perceive the divine, help you to put into practice that which can heal.

Do not judge nor criticize, it is but human frailty to judge in haste the actions of others, but the spiritual way is to remain quiet and loving. You are spirit first, learn to manifest this. You are divine.

Your master and angels ceaselessly labour for you, they do not get angry nor do they judge nor criticize for they know God's law, the plan for unfolding the grand plan of God within man.

The young in spirit are quick to judge, but the elders are patient. They do not expect too much so do not criticize for this is the cause of disintegration of your own being in your life. Instead look with love on those whom your karma has brought you into association.

When man releases the God spark within he makes all things new. This is when he begins to see beauty instead of ugliness, love instead of hate, releasing health instead of sickness. The world becomes fresh and new just as the rain cleanses.

It is easy to dwell on the rough exterior of men. Look beneath, cut away the debris, there you will discover a gentle and beautiful being sleeping. Look always for the prince or princess within. You all possess this sleeping beauty, therefore deal with each other lovingly, forget the hurt and hate, always seek the best, encourage beauty in every way.

*P*urify your own physical atoms with correct thinking, right speech, right actions, right living. Do not judge then you will know happiness untold, of that which you have not dreamed, this will open your prison door, the self imposed prison setting you free.

Forgive as you wish to be forgiven, these words come to you with love, they will help you when you feel troubled or in difficulties. When your emotions threaten to overwhelm you just forgive and all will be forgiven and you will be blest with love.

Do you know what forgiveness means? You yourself your own personality needs forgiveness, though your spirit is divine, you have to learn to overcome. Your personality remains human and needs the forgiveness of your spirit.

As you learn to forgive your personality, so do you learn to forgive your fellow man for seeming errors. Train yourself then, my child, to think in terms of love and forgiveness in all of your life, feel a most beautiful healing take place in you.

Know in the presence of the master your anger and resentment dissolves, you will have a feeling of peace as you are overcome with adoration and love. So then you are pulled above the antagonisms of the earthly plane.

Rising within you is the gentle love, the true light causing you to look on the world with understanding and compassion respecting all. When you truly respect your fellow man so do you respect his life in all ways, generating the love light within that you must live by.

So what if your work does not seem to develop as you wish. Do not get despondent or disheartened, just know and be thankful for you are being prepared; undergoing an initiation for greater work. For no great work can be accomplished without patient preparation. Show patience in all things for every detail of a spirit's work must be done perfectly, be patient with all happenings in your daily life, show patience to your fellow man.

Fear not and be thankful, know your every need is being taken care of. If you are thankful, then you drive out fear. Do not worry about what is ahead, the journey ahead is assured. Have you not been brought forth so far in spite of all fears. Have you not travelled safely through all the trials, sorrows and tribulations of life. You never walk alone. Look back only to recognize the beauty you left behind, do not regret the past, bless it for had you not travelled by that path you would not be here.

All human nature is governed by divine law, the great plan perfect in its outworking. The purpose being to draw all mankind into the one consciousness of God. You are continually moving, travelling to the ultimate happiness before you. Remain steadfast.

Nothing happens by chance know this. We know of the sorrows and trouble of your mortal life, this we fully understand. It is because you personally do not see far enough the road you must travel, you allow yourself to become overcome with anxiety.

God knows your every need. He is within you, have angels who are always active they do not sleep and they do uplift humanity. The evolution of the human race pushes forward, see always the progress, recognize the beauty and the good. Do not become pessimistic, be a bearer of happiness and joy.

No need for fear and anxiety, know you are safely in the hands of the great spirit be strengthened in your heart for what lies before you.

Trust love and love will flow through your whole being. It is easy to look back and say, "How could I have doubted". Have confidence in your guidance. Looking back you will notice there was nothing you could have altered.

Have faith my child there are things you cannot control nor change. But you can change your attitude and accept; knowing you are safe, you are being cared for.

So things do not always work out as you perceive. Know then there is a greater plan. Accept, know the world is your oyster, all things work out for the good in the light.

Do not fear poverty, do you lack the necessary items of life are you not always fed, are you undressed? Fear not for the great spirit does not fail you he knows all too well your every need. He does not let you down, it is you who deprive yourself, forgetting the source from which all things come.

So maybe you feel all goes wrong, do not let it trouble you, let it run its course but be mindful that you keep your vision in the light. Laugh. It passes and all things will come right.

My child I am only too aware of your hardships and disappointments, do not let fear possess you do not succumb, remember you are being tested. We are your angels and you need to be tested. Walk tall.

So the physical body fails you, you may not be as fit and perfect as you could be or deserve. Do you not think we know these things, so maybe material things can become irksome and tiresome. We are well attuned to this and absorb your feelings.

So there are problems and difficulties, be reassured if you truly follow and trust with all your heart, all will be well. All works out as it should, just recognize this and believe.

Do not be troubled unduly by mundane things for when you dwell on earthly troubles, your vibrations become twisted, knotted. Life is not meant for you to dwell on these things. Loosen the knots for when your vibrations are crossed you send out twisted signals like different colour rays criss-crossing over the universe.

Be still let your problems be seen for then we can help. Remember we see what is before you but when your signals become crossed you mix all together. There is only but one true moment and this is now. You are never alone acknowledge the divine within, let God's light shine forth.

Know for sure God is love. Love is light. Light is life. For the one who recognizes the God love, all things work out for the good.

As the divine law operates through the evolution of human kind, then the beautiful purpose of the divine can be brought to fruition. Do not be disturbed or overdriven by petty things. Speak to your master, ask for guidance and help. Be the master of your being, rule your life with love, truth, wisdom and beauty.

I gently advise you not to pay too much attention to earthly matters, though I do not suggest you neglect your earthly duties. Get a better, clearer understanding of the relative values of the spiritual and earthly things. There is much you consider important to you that is not.

Aim to be still, maintain a peaceful spirit then you will find the windows of your soul will open, allowing the eternal light to pour forth absorbing the anxieties you hold close.

Be mindful of the tenderness of your master, he understands and knows your every need, your difficulties and your disappointments. Listen as he calls to come, my child, rise above the turmoil and I will show you the inner peace you do crave. For within your very being lies the inner peace and healing, there need be no fear.

Feel God's love pouring into your being as you relax for it is only then you recognize the beauty within. Concentrate on God's beauty that surrounds you, feel the love pouring through you and to you. Trust me my child for only good can come to you if you but stop feeling anxious.

Become as a little flower, be calm get on with life quietly. Open up your heart to the light of God's love, for the answer of your own hidden problem lies in the surrendering all to God, the God within ever present. Be still. Remain calm.

Save your energy and learn to control the wastage you send out through emotional turmoil and mental expenditure forever taking place in daily life. Be as your master who has learned the supreme lesson, he does not waste energy, the God light within. Learn to remain tranquil and calm be at peace despite the storm of life.

My dear child do not be in such a hurry. Spiritual life does not rip through life like a storm, it never hurries. Be patient do not expect things to happen immediately, there is no hurry you have all eternity. Live, love and be joyful

Ah my child how easy it is to trouble oneself with trivial happenings, becoming emotionally upset with conditions that do not suit. It is easy if you adjust your pace and let the light grow stronger. Let it teach you to control passions and emotions. Keep it stilled and in the right place, for then that particular emotion can be used for spiritual service. Allow it not to storm through the soul disturbing and shattering it.

*D*o not live in fear looking for this or that to happen, as I always say I remind you once more, the future is now, eternity is now, there is no past or present, it all happens now, all is within the embrace of your spirit. It is your reaction to now that is your future. No more anticipation, live for today let the map unfold gradually for it is now.

*Y*ou know it is possible to attain tranquillity of mind under any conditions my child. So you long to be free, live a life of happiness; joyful and healthy. We give to you some things to remember; first my child seek that your spirit remain tranquil, do not be disturbed again. I tell you do not jangle your wires, for from your soul come fibres of light and colours, worrying crosses these, the very source of life, this is why things seem so difficult. Keep your wires free, your contact clear, as a master is never perturbed, he is tranquil and serene.

From the realm of light we see all men are tranquil with shining faces. All work is being executed perfectly, every effort is applied to further the happiness of the community. Know that you have the ability to live likewise on earth.

Oh, please do not excuse yourself by saying that you are human, for we know truly man is divine. My child, when you feel overwhelmed and harassed by affairs of the world, stop and be still. Remember it is but the human part of you that is being tried and tested, know also there exists a higher self.

Feel the infinite love, the infinite power flowing into you. Recognize the glorious colours and lights that surround you, then you will be conscious of a self which is limitless.

Let your inner calm grow, nurture it daily, link yourself with meditation and prayers, let the light shine from your spirit, not depression, only light.

Tread patiently your path, be humble, it is then you will be the recipient of the unfailing power and love, reflecting the divine love of God within.

Remember to hand back to God what you are not able to handle, do your best then hand it back, for the rest is not yours to handle, it will be worked out for you.

You are on a journey to a beautiful garden spread out above you, the eternal garden of the spirit. It is from here we reach out to you, ever ready to assist you. To lift you above the limitations of grief and strife, bringing you home to eternal bliss; from that heavenly life you have all come from and back to which you shall return.

First you must learn to look for the kingdom within, the peaceful place of quiet and stillness. Be serene, maintain the highest level which you are capable, and let the higher influences pour into you, re-creating for the salvation of all mankind.

My child, I wish you to know you are a channel. God waits for you to serve in this way, to help mankind on his path knowing whence it comes from, recognizing the love it sends, for behind you is a power beyond your comprehension.

Let the channel be opened wide so letting the true light flood through, for by your mental direction it goes forth to heal the nations. As you help just one person, so you help the world.

My dear, at any given moment you may be called upon for the master's service. Maybe not in a way you are expecting, for at times you may not even realise that you are being used for the master, but keep your heart open, your channel clear, for you know not when you may be called.

Do not rely on your own strength, through that you limit yourself. Look to the light, the divine love of God, knowing in there lies your strength and your angel will always be untiring in your work.

Look to the light knowing all your needs are being catered for, it is not you alone that serves. Remain firm, calm, strong yet humble, remain in love.

The most important thing is to let the light shine forth continually, thus you remain open for the master's service in order to fulfil the small tasks he places at your disposal. Patiently working in your own little space, you will be greatly rewarded for your services by remaining aware of the ever presence of your invisible companions and angels.

It matters not what your purpose or work is, what does matter is how you apply yourself. Do it with all your love, strength and conscience. Ask for wisdom that you may perform in the right manner, and for ever increasing courage and strength that you do not become faint hearted and falter along the way.

*W*e are always looking for you to be ready to be used as a channel to send forth the love and light around you. Be ever ready, hold tight to all around you, the beautiful, true and good. Do not become negative, remain positive in all ways thus turning your mind to messengers from other worlds who look to you to respond.

I offer you peace and tranquillity, may it be yours forever. For if you lift yourself to the God within, the very heart of you, so do you lift the whole universe. Even the earth beneath betters itself.

See and accept the responsibility we place upon you. Do not allow darkness and negativity to deny your birthright, my child, that of happiness and freedom; that of service and worship. What a most magnificent opportunity is placed before you, deny it not.

Dwelling continually on God's love within, is your own personal contribution to the greatest plan of all times. Perform it well, recognizing only the goodness in every man, accepting God's presence everywhere. Train yourself to look always to the light and this is yours all along the way.

Recognizing the goodness and love within is the greatest task put to any man, for God is within all. Teaching this to all men is to replace darkness with light in even the most ignorant on earth.

My child you cannot, must not, do the work of another for each and everyone has a different task that must be done and each must do their own. By all means be there for them, help them to accept that which is theirs and ask for help, for this too, they must learn is there for the asking. Teach them to ask from the centre of their being, and have not fear about the strength or power needed to do their task.

Lift up your head, make eye contact with those around. Walk tall for none is greater than thee, remain sure footed on the ground, raise your head above.

Your feet will be guided on the right path, fear not for love surrounds you. Be tranquil of mind as you surrender to the light, have confidence and let your heart be full of love, for peace is yours. Let wisdom be your guide.

It is time to discard the bondage you have placed yourself in, discard the chains and see yourself as you truly are. Allow yourself to be uplifted. It matters not how difficult your path, seek only the God life. Be lifted as on eagles wings to your higher realms, as some may say in your imagination.

Come my child into the bountiful light knowing it is recreating a force to flow through you, the source of true light. Let it flow through you, strengthening the weak, and healing that which needs to be healed. See the crooked made straight for man is but spirit. Does not spirit conquer matter?

For you to be a bearer of light to the whole world, step forth with confidence. Let it truly shine through, quickening the earth's vibrations, healing and blessing as it pours forth.

There is no need to use force in any condition, wait and the strength will be given to you to face any condition; so you may face any task given to you. I must comfort you when I say any experience, however distasteful, no matter how it hurts, is doing good for the whole world, if you can meet such tasks and testing with tranquillity. Trust my child let love be your guide.

Sacrifices must be made in order to adequately serve the needs of the world. Did not a great master demonstrate this to us? For my child true service is not given without a sacrifice. So you may pull back, this does not alter anything, for the law of life must be adhered to. Let love possess your heart, then the service rendered will bring great joy, so as to outweigh any sacrifice.

Be thankful to the call of service for whatever you do, no matter how menial the task while in your physical being, is a form of service. Undertake to do it well, give it your all, it is your special task and through this you contribute to the happiness of mankind.

Remain trusting, no matter what your problem or task may be, know you have the guidance and help of loving angels who have been appointed to you. Do not place a problem in our hands and then try to solve it. Let trust, real trust, activate. Your angels do not let you down, know they work in God's light, the light of love.

Be firm, practice not letting your body and brain do what it chooses; be mindful you are in control, let love guide you. Use the light in all situations, and see how things that trouble no longer remain a problem.

If you hand over a problem, let us solve it, do not interfere. Listen, be aware you are being cared for, there is no need to force the issue if things are not to your liking. Sit back, evaluate, for something better is on its way. Be patient my child let love be your guide.

Be as a flower open up gently, do not be in a hurry, be patient, practice seeing the master overhead in a gathering. He is ever present. Haste not regarding spiritual matters.

One step at a time is all that is needed, time matters not. Remain sure in your heart, the opportunity comes to you to do the master's work.

If things do not work out as you wish, know something better is at hand. Trust and know that love is the one true path, love and forgiveness.

As the love increases within, remain tranquil and calm for wisdom is given to you.

*T*o find the centre of truth, go within for all knowledge dwells within the centre of your heart. Meditate and go within, draw from the stream of knowledge. The answer lies within, you should think with your inner mind, intuition. The way to truth is to be in contact with the spirit, for outside remains chaos, the material world of substance.

Do not continue to think with the human mind, to do so is to bog yourself down, continually looking outside for the answer when all the time it lies within, in your very being.

Always see the good in all things, even if the darkest side is what is shown to you. There remains the good to be recognized. Look with unconditional love, and you cannot fail.

Do not hide your thoughts of love and good will. Such love should be broadcasted for you know not what good you do simply by allowing your higher self to be the ruler of your life.

Allow the light to flow through you and quicken the light of the fellow man. Do not look back on the troubles or problems presented to you that have been of a disturbance to you. Be mindful of the ever presence of the light, knowing God is working through you for the good of mankind.

Look for the underlying principles, not for the purely personal solutions. You must seek the good of the whole, not the partial, for if you lay your problems by the thought of your master, a solution will be given to you.

Rise above the lower vibrations, and look at your problems as a whole. See them with the eyes of a spirit, and you will be surprised how different they look.

*Think only good, do not be pessimistic.
Exchange thoughts of trouble with
thoughts of good.*

Though to you your fellow man is not striving towards God, look and see that it is what he does. Notice how the whole world is becoming more spiritual

All that is asked of you is that you strive to do your best. Who are you to judge if you appear to make mistakes. Doing your best is your surety that you are doing the right thing, even if this is not apparent to you. Do your best, thus being a service to all mankind.

You cannot err for you serve in the light of the master. If you doubt, remain still and wait, when doubt dissipates move forward with courage. Be still as the light disperses the clouds around you, then move forward with courage.

Be not demanding and impatient, be trusting for you may not recognise the particular path you tread. Remember your angels are there for you. Have confidence and know not fear.

If you do not know which way to go, stand still, let it be shown to you and you will see change in conditions around you, and all will be well. Do not force, for you create a tangle by being over eager to get on. If you have to retrace your steps, you fall into a muddle, be still and trust in the ever presence of God.

Remember there are no accidents, all happens at the right time. Time is irrelevant in the grand scale, there are no mistakes. You may not always remember this, my child, but if you follow the guidance of the spirit all things will be made plain to you.

$\mathcal{S}$ometimes you may need to seek outside help, know that this too is shown to you, though at times it is not clear to you. Know this, if man should fail, God never does.

You are a child of light, walk tall and live in your spirit, let nothing hold you back. It is always easy to be cheerful and happy when things are going well, not so easy when things seem difficult. So simple to return kindness for kindness, love for love. This means little, you must be able to rise above and do this at all times.

So your karma brings sorrows and anxieties. Fear not, have faith and courage for others look to you to see the light shining forth, maybe unconsciously, they still do, for they know you have something special which is helpful and good.

Remember, let the light continue shining in your heart and mind for a great privilege has been given you to help all mankind, leading him onward, towards the greatest of all.

Remember always as inside the oyster shell lies the pearl, inside you lies the pearl of eternal light and love. Let it shine forth, do not shut it in. Only you can do this, no one can do it for you, we can but assist.

Open your heart, let it be free and know only good can come of it. For as you reach in you are able to soar like an eagle to the highest realms being made available to you.

Spread the word of love, joy and peace and it shall be yours. For this is the source of true life that we must freely live by, to know the true meaning of life.

Let God's light shine forth around you and in you, let it spread throughout all the universe.

You see the pearl was never meant to be hidden permanently, nor is the love. The true meaning of love is to be spread for all to learn, it is the purest of energies.

Just remember let true love be your guide, love of yourself, your fellow man, in fact the whole universe. To love is to live in God's pure light.

How to Contact Your Angels

Meditating and contacting your angels can sometimes be frustrating but that is usually because you think that they are going to speak to you in words or suddenly appear to you in a vision. These occurrences are quite rare. Generally your angels speak to you when you least expect it, or in times of greatest need.

However if you wish to develop a technique for contacting your angels, and we all have them, then you can use the following meditation to open up those lines of communication. This particular meditation I use with my students when helping them reach their higher self, angels or guides of light.

You can use this meditation to either gain some insight into where you are spiritually or seek specific help. Remember that your angels are there to help you spiritually, not increase your material possessions. If this happens as a result of your spiritual endeavours this is fine, but should not be your primary goal in life.

If you decided to use this meditation with a friend, then give them some questions you would like to ask and have them read them out when you have contacted your angels or guides. Alternatively you can have a pen and paper handy and when you feel the messages coming through you can write them down. If using this method write down the first thoughts that come to mind, even if they sound foolish. Sometimes we have to *unplug* the conscious thoughts to allow the flow of higher consciousness.

Just a small note of caution, you will not receive messages from the light if you are in a state of anxiety, fear or other strong negative emotion. Following what my angels and guides have taught me I will be encouraging you to challenge any first contact to establish that it is a message from the light. Once you start communicating allow yourself to be calm and be prepared to accept whatever the angels feel is right for you at this time.

The messages usually come in thought, image or by impressions (sensations). Sometimes there is just an overwhelming feeling of love or other uplifting emotion. Sometimes an impression of colour. Any of these could be your angels contacting you.

You can also use this meditation in any of the following ways:

· Get together with a group of friends and have one of them read it out to the others, or

· Record these words onto a tape and then play it to yourself during a time of quiet, or

· Read it in passages and then close your eyes allowing the suggestions to become real.

Where you see the ellipses (...) pause for a moment then proceed. Speak slowly and without too much fluctuation in the voice. Use music for background if you wish.

Take a deep breath in, note any tensions you may be holding and breath them out...and again deep breath in ... note any remaining tensions and then breath them out. One more time breath in ... breath out and relax. Continue breathing in your normal manner and allow that with every breath that you take you become more and more relaxed ... more and more relaxed ... more and more relaxed.

Allow yourself now to be within the glow of the beautiful white light ... light that is warm and loving ... soft and gentle. Allow this beautiful light to permeate through every cell in your body, every fibre

of your being, every level of your consciousness. Feel the beautiful light bring peace and love to your whole being.

Allow the light to gently quieten the thoughts...the chatter of everyday life. Feel the light move down your head to throat and neck...releasing all the tensions held there. Allow the light to move through your shoulders washing away all the burdens you may be carrying. Feel the loving light move down your arms to your hands and fingertips...release whatever you may be holding that you no longer need.

Allow the light to move into your chest...breath it into your lungs...let it wash through your heart bringing peace and joy...let it move through your abdomen...allow the light to restore harmony in this area of assimilation...feel the light move down your legs to your feet and toes allowing that every step that you take is a step of love and light.

Allow yourself to be drawn up into this beautiful light ...higher and higher...higher and higher until you reach a place of beautiful golden light...a place that is warm and loving...safe and comfortable. And in this place of peace and harmony I would like you now to visualise seeing before you a beautiful golden door surrounded by the safe and gentle golden light.

In a moment you will be invited to go through

that door and meet the loving angels and beings of light that are with you all the time. Remember that these loving entities can present themselves in any way - in a recognised physical form...as beings of light... sometimes colour...sometimes in a symbolic manner. However your angels and guides present themselves allow yourself to accept them....

Now step forward and open the door...move through the doorway...allow yourself to see, feel or sense the presence of your angel.... When you feel you have contacted one of your angels, in whatever form, ask "In God's name are you from the light". When you are comfortable that the entity you have contacted is from the light...and you will know this by either an overwhelming feeling of love or a definite impression that they have responded by acknowledging they are from the light, then ask "Tell me something I need to know".

Take a moment to listen to the reply and then continue to communicate by asking questions. Listen carefully to the answers being aware that they will answer you literally...and they will always have your spiritual well-being at heart.

(Leave a few moments here to allow time for communication - when ready, continue)

Thank your angels for being here at this time...know that you can return at any time to this beautiful peaceful place...as you leave do not close the door knowing that it is always open, welcoming you back.

Allow yourself to be once again in the beautiful white light...feel its loving energies...bring your focus now back to your physical reality...allow your breathing and heart beat to return to normal...become aware of crystal clarity of mind...feel the energy return to your arms and legs to the point where you may wish to start moving them...and in your own time, when you are ready, take a deep breath - open your eyes...bringing back into this physical reality all the love and wisdom you have allowed yourself to receive.

Whatever you receive from your angels or spirit guides take from it what you need and leave the rest for another time. Messages from your angels of light are timeless and will have as much relevance to you in six or twelve months time as on the day you received them.

Enjoy your journey of learning. Let love and light be your guide.

About the Author

Eileen Goble is a well known psychotherapist, counsellor and holistic teacher with her own practice in Melbourne, Australia. She also runs certificate and diploma courses in metaphysical studies and holistic therapy.

Eileen is the author of *Spirit Guides* and has produced three meditation tapes two of which have interpretative booklets to help you on your spiritual journey. These titles are available in Australia, New Zealand and the United Kingdom.

A popular speaker at mind body and spirit festivals in both Australia and London, Eileen is often invited to be a guest speaker or occasional lecturer for different groups and other interested institutions.

Eileen was born in England, but her family migrated to Australia when she was ten. She lives in Melbourne with her husband, has four children, one grandchild and a spoilt dog called Harry.